Bald Eagles of the Mississippi

LARRY ROGERS

Acknowledgments

Thank you to the following people who inspire me to learn more and make better art. Your companionship makes my work fun.

Eric and Norma Curby

Larry Williams

Burt and Marilyn Gearhart

Michael and Cindy Fitzgerald

Thank you to my partner, Kim Waters, for your encouragement and help with image selections.

Thank you to my son, Bryan, for your inspiration and design guidance.

Other books by Larry Rogers

Getting the Shot: Yellowstone

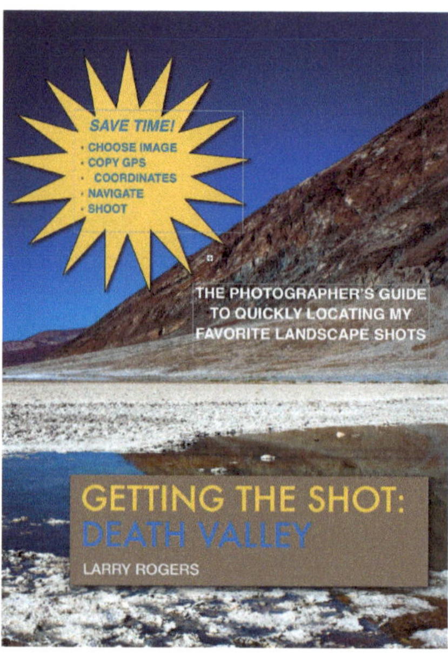

Getting the Shot: Death Valley

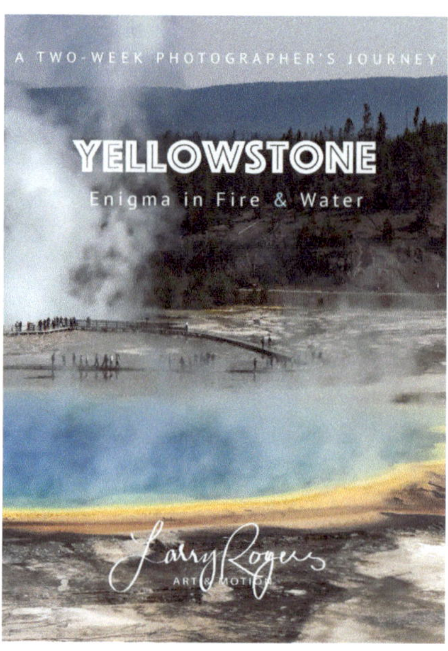

YELLOWSTONE: Enigma in Fire & Water

A very great vision is
needed, and the man who
has it must follow it as the
eagle seeks the deepest
blue of the sky.
Crazy Horse

Migratory Bald Eagles

As the Bald Eagle population in North America continues to recover from near-extinction, reports indicate rising numbers of nesting pairs in almost every state in the United States. This is certainly great news, and a hopeful trend for the future.

In this publication I will focus on birds that comprise a segment of the Bald Eagle population across the North American continent that migrate across vast distances twice each year.

My research has found that eagle migration routes along the east coast of the United States, Canada, Mexico and Central America are reasonably well-documented. Researchers have been banding and attaching GPS tracking devices to migratory birds for several years. Radio transmitters make it possible to track the movements of selected birds. Data they collect is considered to be representative of the general population of migratory Bald Eagles along the east coast.

The adult Bald Eagle shown on the opposite page is carrying a type of tracking device known as a 'backpack,' as well as a leg band. I photographed this bird on January 27, 2018, on the northern Mississippi River. So far, I have not been able to locate any studies or conservation group(s) that are tracking Bald Eagle migration in the central/midwest United States.

This bird, which I'll call 'Backpack,' has been fitted with a transmitter and yet it was seen in the north central US. It may have strayed from an eastern group, or there may be a conservation group that is tracking migration in the central USA. I will continue looking for more information on migration routes through the central part of the continent for a future update.

Universities and conservation groups are learning and sharing more about the reasons behind animal migration. In the case of Bald Eagles pictured in this publication, there is certainly a strong possibility that seasonal temperature changes are a major factor. We know that significant populations of Bald Eagles are found in Canada and Alaska during summer, and that the primary diet of this population (fish, small game, and carrion) is in short supply during winter months, as waterways freeze and snowfall covers much of the open land.

Migration is thought to be a key contributor to the general health of wildlife populations through reduction of in-breeding. Scientists have postulated that elk and pronghorn populations in the western United States underwent population decline as human expansion and development encroached on migration routes these animals had been using for hundreds or thousands of years. Very recently, conservation groups have completed projects to construct wildlife bridges over highways and replace lower-strand barbed wire with smooth wire on rach land fences. Research indicates that these animal populations are now recovering.

Birds pictured in this publication can be found on the northern Mississippi River from December through early February in most years. Several websites report numbers of birds seen near waterways and landmarks where they are known to congregate.

"Backpack": An eagle working for conservation

I first saw this bird in January 2018, fishing near a dam on the northern Mississippi River. It has been fitted with a GPS tracking device and leg band. Conservation organizations use data collected from birds like "Backpack" to better understand the life they lead and the risks they face.

Bald Eagle on the Hunt: Soaring

The 'soaring' Maneuver

In the photo on the opposite page, you see a beautiful adult Bald Eagle soaring high above the waters of the Mississippi River. When I see a bird doing this, I try to notice whether or not it is constantly looking down. If so, it may be hunting or locked onto a potential food target. Watch closely, and get your camera ready - the transition from hunting to the attack happens quickly!

Be wary of 'Eagle Days'

Until roughly ten years ago, my photography concentrated on landscapes and western wildlife (bears, moose, elk, etc). I was very interested in photographing Bald Eagles and other large raptors, but 'eagle days' just didn't seem to pan out for me.

Two 'eagle day' events are still burned in my memory, and I will share these experiences with you because I want you to do your research better than I did. The first of my negative experiences happened more than ten years ago, when I read an ad for 'Cayuga Power Station Eagle Days,' referring to a plant now operated by Duke Energy in Vermillion County, Indiana.

The people hosting the event were very nice. They were well prepared to receive visitors, but there were no eagles to see. I may have seen a speck in the distance, but that was it. A similar thing happened a year later. I drove from southern Ohio to Tennessee to attend an 'Eagle Day' on Dale Hollow Lake, only to freeze all day long on a boat ride around the lake. I was able to witness a possible Bald Eagle dive-bomb a group of coots on the lake, but I didn't get any usable photos.

Go where the Eagles are

With that as background, I'll share what I have learned about eagle watching and photographing. You may hear about nesting eagles, and while these birds may be around more days each year than migratory birds, the challenge is they are really hard to spot. Most bald eagle nests have been protected by blocking access to their locations. Migratory eagles, in comparison, can be spotted in large numbers as they congregate around areas where they find food in winter - open water in the vicinity of power plant cooling towers, or locks and dams on major rivers, like the Mississippi.

To get great photos, consider factors like wind direction (you want the wind at your back so the birds will be flying toward you as they capture fish). Another big factor is the distance from where you can set up your camera and tripod to open water being fished by the eagles. The longer the distance, the longer the lens needed. Finally, evaluate obstructions - fences or walls may obstruct your view.

Shooting Tips

I recommend a DSLR camera that supports interchangeable lenses. Photos seen in this publication were shot with a super telephoto lens, but a lens with 200 mm focal length or longer will often produce usable photos. I typically use a shutter speed of 1/1600 sec, any aperture, and ISO as low as needed to enable the 1/1600 sec shutter speed. As with all photography situations, light direction is a key, and good camera technique goes a long way toward getting great images. Keep practicing!

Previous:
Adult migratory Bald Eagle, carrying a "Backpack" GPS tracking device and leg band

Opposite:
Adult migratory Bald Eagle soars above the northern Mississippi River

Bald Eagle on the Hunt

Eagles are raptors: Birds of prey

All of the Bald Eagles pictured in this publication are migratory birds. In many cases, these images show common predatory behavior of the birds. After a long migration in search of food, the hunt is an extremely serious activity. It is not uncommon to observe two or more birds fighting over a catch. Juvenile birds are not as good at hunting as adults, and will commonly resort to fighting over catch with an adult carrying a catch.

The Hunt: A Sequence of flight transition phases (images on pages 11, 12-13)

Over the next several pages, I will discuss the process I have observed as an adult Bald Eagle makes the transition from level flight (soaring) to the hover, followed by attack mode, catch mode, and then returns to the roost to consume a well-deserved meal. The image on page 11 (opposite) shows the hover. The image on pages 12-13 is a collage of five frames taken from a continuous burst of 20 frames, captured on February 5, 2017, showing the transition from the hover (right, opposite page) into the 'dive' onto the target in the Mississippi River below.

The 'Hover' maneuver

In the photo on the opposite page, you see a beautiful adult Bald Eagle just after spotting a potential meal in the Mississippi River below. Notice how the wings are partially folded - it's a fluttering motion that holds the bird 'suspended' while it determines if the target is actually worth diving upon. Most often, in my experience, the decision is made to attack the prey.

The 'dive' maneuver

Please refer to the two-page spread on pages 14-15. The attack in this sequence is from right-to-left. The sequence starts out at low speed but accelerates very quickly. In the last (leftmost) frame, the bird is entering its final 'glide' mode which it will hold until the last possible moment before the 'catch.'

The 'Catch, Secure the Catch and Out-fly the Bandit' maneuvers

These are self-explanatory. Full-page images are found on pages 16, 18, 20, 22 and 24, respectively.

Notes on Equipment and Technique for Photographing birds in flight

This is an exciting time to be a wildlife photographer. The latest camera gear is setting new standards for portability, image quality, and image frame rate, all of which are important in capturing any moving wildlife and critical for capturing birds in flight. All of the images in this publication were captured using a full-frame DSLR (digital single-lens reflex) camera, with a super telephoto lens (600 mm), and teleconverter (1.4 x). The latest digital mirrorless cameras are great choices, too. The most important features in a camera for bird photography are manually adjustable shutter speed (typically 1/1600 sec), burst mode (at least 5 frames per sec), and telephoto lens (up to 200 mm or longer).

Previous, pages 8-9:
Juvenile migratory Bald Eagle soars above the northern Mississippi River

Opposite:
Adult migratory Bald Eagle slows to a hover over the northern Mississippi River

Bald Eagle on the Hunt: Transition from Hover to Dive

Bald Eagle on the Hunt: The Dive

Bald Eagle on the Hunt: The Dive

Bald Eagle on the Hunt: The Attack

Bald Eagle on the Hunt: The Catch

Bald Eagle on the Hunt: Secure The Catch

Bald Eagle on the Hunt: Out-fly the Bandit

Beyond the Click

An Invitation

Now that you have read about my adventure on the northern Mississippi River, watching and photographing wild migratory Bald Eagles, I invite you to think about what will come next for you.

Will you go out to experience wild migratory birds, like the Bald Eagles seen here? If so, will you use any of the planning or photo tips in this publication? I hope you will! In preparation for that, I have a few final thoughts.

Artist, explorer, or both?

I invite you to consider how you want to experience your next exploration or adventure. There is no right or wrong way to experience wildlife or a wild place, but there are very different experiences to be had. I, for example, consider myself an 'artist' whose brush is a camera, whose paint is a computer and software, and whose canvas is the print media upon which my visual art will be seen and, I hope, enjoyed by others.

I am also an 'explorer.' In fact, I was an explorer before I became an artist, as I traveled abroad for military service as a young man. That experience opened my mind to the realization that the world is a larger and even more wonderful collection of experiences than I had previously imagined. These experiences are available for everyone to enjoy. Tragically, too few of us actually have these experiences, for a variety of reasons.

My "why," the reasons I explore and share

I explore and share my experiences so that other people might be inspired to do things and see places they may not otherwise do and see. A few of those people who are inspired to see and enjoy wild places may even become future stewards, which is a vision that inspires me to embark on even more adventures and share them with others, like you.

The medium I have chosen for sharing my message is the printed word, illustrated with works of art that I generate from a digital camera and illustrate on the printed page or, in some cases, on exquisite fine art paper or special metal print surfaces. With that said, it would be a disservice to you, the reader, if I stopped with that over-simplified description. In the interest of fairness and full disclosure, there is much more to the story of how these images are made.

Before and after the click

This publication shares the story and images from two separate trips to the northern Mississippi River between Illinois and Iowa in January 2018, but the truth is, I have made trips to the same region many times in the years leading up to the 2018 trips. In addition, I started planning the specific places I would visit and photograph several weeks prior to the trip.

Photographing migratory wildlife is different from photographing landscapes. In the case of Bald Eagles during winter migration, weather conditions are possibly the most important consideration. It is important to have cold weather and complete snow cover, so that eagles will look for fish in unfrozen water, which you can find near dams or power plant cooling tower outflows.

We travel by car so that we can take an extensive set of equipment with us (lenses, filters, tripods, batteries, and incidental tools).

To the Artist: The click is only the beginning

Communication is the artist's objective. My objective is to share the feeling I had when I stood at a place or located an animal. I never have forgotten the sensory experience of a moment that moved me - a diving Bald Eagle coming right at me, or an eagle carrying a heavy fish while trying to out-fly another hungry bird.

For my fellow photographers desiring to connect with your audience, in my experience, communication through imagery is not a function of technical perfection. Sharpness, saturation and contrast are not as important as your composition and imact of the scene. I like to visit some places over and over, and I try to get images that evoke different emotional reactions. The interaction of a momma Grizzly with her cubs, or eagles on the hunt will evoke different reactions in the viewer.

Art is about emotion

All images shown in this publication have been processed using software that enables me to 'shape' the image in such a way that it helps me recall how I felt when I captured it. I often think back to a time when I was first learning digital photography. I would go someplace hoping to get stunning images like those I saw online or in photo books, but I failed every time, because I had not yet become an artist.

Before I share an image in print, I process it in a way that will evoke emotion in my reader. My photo tips are intended to be helpful, but the truth is, most people will not have invested the time and expense that I have - the pursuit of excellence takes time. Just know that your images are your own - you were there!

Forever a student

Anyone willing to take the artist's journey can match or exceed the image 'quality' seen in this or any other publication. Yes, you can! Let me share a few tips to get your started on your journey:

Be forever a student
> Study everything about your subjects
> Ask questions
> Listen to what others have to say
> Share
> Experiment

Learn what "style" is, and develop yours

Know "why" you make art and commit to it

Be disciplined

Question everything you do

Make good art, and only good art

Closing thoughts

I have shared this story and my images in the hope that you will be inspired get outside and have your own experiences. Your experience will be yours to remember. Some of you may want to share your experiences, and I hope I have given that group some ideas and an interest in inspiring others do things and see places they might otherwise miss. All my best to you!

Larry Rogers

Next:
About the author

About the Author

Larry Rogers has been photographing national parks and wildlife for more than 40 years. Formally educated in electrical engineering and computer science, Larry was given his first camera around age 8 and cannot recall a time when he did not have a camera.

Following graduation from college, he served as an Air Defense Officer in the US Army, a US government civilian employee and small business owner. But, throughout, his passion for wildlife, wild places, and the environment fueled his love of photography and the arts.

With a burning passion to constantly learn and develop his art to a high level, Larry is now extending his art to new perspectives, flying a drone and publishing books which he hopes will inspire the next generation of conservation and nature photographers.

He currently lives in southwest Ohio, in the United States. He is the father of two sons, and grandfather to two granddaughters.

Larry welcomes readers to follow and/or contact him via social media, email or comments on his website.

Contact

Instagram: larryrogersartandmotion
LinkedIn: linkedin.com/in/the-conservancy-project
email: inquire@larryrogers.us
Twitter: @larryrogers
Website: larryrogersphotography.us

More from Larry Rogers

eBooks are available on the iBooks Store:

Getting the Shot: Yellowstone
Getting the Shot: Death Valley

Art prints are available at larryrogersphotography.us

Yellowstone Landscapes
Yellowstone Wildlife
Grand Teton National Park
and many more galleries

Follow us on Instagram for up-to-date information on new products and current projects.

Be safe in your travels, and remember, "Take only photographs, and leave only footprints!"